# DAMAGES

# Damages

*Elaine Terranova*

COPPER CANYON PRESS

Publication of this book is supported by a grant from the National Endowment for the Arts and a grant from the Lannan Foundation. Additional support to Copper Canyon Press has been provided by the Andrew W. Mellon Foundation, the Lila Wallace–Reader's Digest Fund, and the Washington State Arts Commission. Copper Canyon Press is in residence with Centrum at Fort Worden State Park.

Library of Congress Cataloging-in-Publication Data
Terranova, Elaine.
Damages / by Elaine Terranova.
p. cm.
ISBN 1-55659-105-5 (pbk.)
I. Title.
PS3570.E6774D36 1995
811'.54 – dc20                                    95-32462

## COPPER CANYON PRESS

P.O. BOX 271, PORT TOWNSEND, WASHINGTON 98368

# ACKNOWLEDGMENTS

Grateful acknowledgment is given to the magazines in which earlier versions of these poems appeared:

"Amusement Park" (*Passaic County Community College 1990 Anthology*, 2nd prize)

"Badgers" (*River Styx*, no. 41, 1995)

"Black Narcissus" (*The American Poetry Review*, vol. 21/no. 6, November/December, 1992)

"The Cardinal" (*Sycamore Review*, vol. 1/no. 1, Spring 1989)

"The Choice" (*Confrontation*, no. 46/47, Fall 1991/Winter 1992)

"Death Site" (*North Essex Review*, Spring 1993)

"In the Bindery" (*Slipstream*, 1992)

"The Line" (*Boulevard*, Spring 1992)

"The Mad School" (*The American Poetry Review*, vol. 21/no. 6, November/December, 1992)

"Phobia" (*The American Poetry Review*, vol. 21/no. 6, November/December, 1992)

"The Spell" (forthcoming, *River Styx*, no. 41, 1995)

"Sports Photographer" (*Aethlon*, no. VII, Spring 1990)

"Story in the Style of Henry James" (*The Cream City Review*, Spring, 1993)

"Strawberry Fête" (*North Essex Review*, Spring 1993)

"Ten Years Old" (*Sycamore Review*, vol. 4/no. 2, 1992)

"Their House" (*The New Yorker*, June 10, 1991)

and to New American Radio which produced "Taking Tap at Miss Paterson's" for the radio in 1990.

The author also wishes to thank the Tyrone Guthrie Centre in Ireland and the Ragdale Foundation for residencies during which some of these poems were written.

I am grateful as well to friends for their comments, especially Jeanne Murray Walker, Darcy Cummings, and Jack Israel, and to Sylvia S. Cooperman for her support.

*To Lee H. Cooperman*

# CONTENTS

I

II

III

# DAMAGES

I

# PHOBIA

Because from the tour bus
I could not hear even the cries of vendors,
only staring out at brilliant tinware
and pottery set up on stands,
the occasional geranium unfurling
on the windowsill of crumbling,
whitewashed housefronts,
how should I know when not to look?

As the bus turns I witness
that starburst of frazzled flight,
a startled chicken scratching up dirt.
The comb and wattles are like
congealed blood. Behind the glass
my limbs are jerking in response.
I feel the sharp beak, the talons digging in.

In my mouth is a taste
of decomposing food. My husband
can't think what to do. I am a person
in a dream. And yet he sees
the sickness and the sweat are real.
He reaches out his hand as my mother
must once have reached out hers,
a link to any possibility.

My mother who so loved birds,
who chattered to them as she chattered
to me. I fetched her a crippled starling once,
frail and speckled, a rival heartbeat
in my hand. She fed it milk-soaked bread
till it was black and sleek, till it would fly up
and sit, a dark sign, on her shoulder.
But that is not what troubled me. It was only

the wings beating like something
that will not be settled in life.

At the hotel that night, still feverish,
I draw between my thumb and middle finger
the cool satin ribbon that trims
the pillow slip. I press my wedding band
to my mouth as if to quiet it, but overhead
the whir of the ceiling fan
wrenches me back again and again from sleep
with its frantic wings.

# THE MAD SCHOOL

I.

We teachers boost ourselves
up onto the low stone wall, our backs
to the outside. Someone has scattered
cow bones in the grass. It's how
these children learn, stumbling
across their lessons. Thus Frances,
dropping to the ground, discovers slugs.
A light of beautiful emptiness
comes into her face. Everyone kneels
to help her separate the wet dead dirt
from the live. We set them like small,
shivering mouths into an aquarium
with stones and flags of grass
and bring it in. I never see them move again.

Inside, I press my hand down hard
against the open book and read aloud,
or else just stare with them
through the windows' white-paned cells.
They are trying to hold still.
All it takes is a bell or a voice sounding out
the syllables of words – just the sun
blundering into the room, and soon Irene,
dwarfed and stoic as a fireplug,
begins to sob. Books, blocks, phantoms
are flung into the air. We move fast,
the aide and I, subduing. Once I have to sit on
the small, offending body. Once I sprain my back.

2.

All year I balance on the stone wall,
heels splintering mica. And then it's spring.
The skin splits on a bucket of sour creek water
I'd have turned out in the hallway sink.
A thin, unexpected thing, the new frog leaps.
The children, too, are growing.
But they are asymmetrical in their growth
like trees on a hill that the wind
blows only one way. I walk among them,
watch any one of them, watch the fingers
bend back tensely against what they want to do.
Watch Saul, in the hooded shirt, fierce and delicate
as a fallen angel, far off dragging trash cans
onto the train tracks, waiting for the accident.

Sometimes we take our classes swimming.
What it must mean to them
to leave the stone shoulders of the pool,
trusting to nothing, all their voices
all at once clawing at air.
I can only wade in up to my thighs and stop.

# BLACK NARCISSUS, THE MOVIE

The shadow of the bell
as she rings it
passes across the young nun's face
like the anguish of love,
though at the time
she is wondering who it is
one would or could love.

Mist circles a white mountain.
Her eyes drop to orchids,
rhododendron. Each petal
is an invitation. Each beggar
at the roadside becomes one
of the lost bones of her faith.

Even Reverend Mother,
for all her prayers,
has no rest.
Once love was a fish
that jumped through her blood.
She finds it still
in the head of a snake or a bird's wing,
tiny, vibrant, fuchsia.

And what is not
contaminated by color? Theirs,
anyone's, is a tortured path
up to religion as high and white as this.
To have been sent at all
must be a test. Later,
those left will be lowered
down the mountain in their pride
on squat gray donkeys.

# NEEDLEWORK

Sometimes fate takes
a needle's path through cloth,
looping in and out,
retracing its own stitches,
twisting like a serpent.

In a Moorish seraglio
at Tordesillas, later a convent,
Phillippe, le Bel, kept one woman only,
Juana, his wife, Juana, la Loca,
in a cell with no windows
for forty-nine years.

Daughter of Ferdinand and Isabella,
mother of the Emperor Charles V,
she never stood beneath
the throne room's coffered ceiling,
never drew through her fingers
Phillippe's gift, red-violet tapestries
stiffened with gold.

Here one day Pedro the Cruel
would install his young mistress
and their daughter begin
the long chain of white-robed nuns.

Thyme climbed the hillside then,
as it does now. Sparrows flitted in dust,
scattering anywhere fear sent them.
Within her stone walls
Juana walked off from herself
into flowers and ferns,
past statues with their mouths open.

Each day was a union of light and sense,
her needle stammering through cloth
as trumpet vines vied for her attention
with the bright eyes
in the butterfly's orange wings.

# AMUSEMENT PARK

When the man grips her arm
at Willow Grove Amusement Park,
it will be half a caress.
He will rub his fingers
along the inside of her wrist,
skin so delicate, so seldom touched
it seems unfamiliar even to her.

She and her friend are twelve
and loose as dimes in the world.
They are not themselves.
At the white, ornate gates
they have slid the smiles of grown women
in Tangee across their faces.

The park is wide and dusty.
They make their way through it,
roller coaster, rocket, flying cars.
Ride after ride lifts them
to where the sun breaks
over their tiny remembered earth,
drops them closer than they can stand to it.

Then the cricket that's her pulse
exposes itself, the beat of her own heart.

The two men have coaxed them
toward the trees, all four laced together
in the shadow of leaves. She has
been waiting all her life
for something to touch her. How then
is she able to pull herself loose
from that hand, so urgent, so particular?

# THE CHOICE

It's a fine, rococo thing,
this loneliness. You see
where it circles and builds,
where the body
with upright spine,
keeps it aloft. She could

match her death
to any season. That spring
the sun put a pale hand
on her. Too little,
too late. Like a drowned
person rising to the surface
of a lake, she wasn't fooled.

She looked out the window
over the edge of the earth.
Children were clinging
to a metal kangaroo
in the center of the court.
Around them, lunchers sat,
firm on benches. Sundays,
she listened to the church choir
hold their long whole notes. Everything
had a knack for hanging on.
Even the old refrigerator
by the kitchen table, though it
shook with noise like a train,
wasn't going anywhere.

But in the tailor shop downstairs
where things are made right,

garments were left hanging,
what is human set free again
from the arms of cloth.

# THE LINE

All afternoon,
cows and rough gorse and
sometimes, high up,
antelopes passing secretly
like a tremor under the skin.

This is harsh land,
cold most of the year
but for its crack of light,
its short summer.

Now a step back into dark.
The dim bar has split-leather stools,
a mirror smudged with smoke and dust.
At the clean, white snap of apron
we stare into a girl's scarred face,
then beyond, at the crimped,
dark back of her head
in the mirror.

She is tough, built solid,
a mountainside of longing. Still in school
or maybe that small, good-looking man
with the perm and the fine eyes
making her nervous
is not her father but her husband.

A flash of lightning,
the fault in her cheek,
line between a before and after.
Imprint of the jagged bottle,
sharp stone she struck or windshield,
whatever taught her this lesson.

# A CROWD

– on an exhibit of 139 skulls at the Mütter Museum

As in life the skulls face front,
out of pride or ignorance.
They never turn to one another,
not even this small, eager one
which is yellowing.

On and on they ride
in their doomed elevator

like shells, cleared
of every wish
without a hand to help them,
and anyhow nothing within reach.

They have been picked clean.
Crows are in their eyes
and in the dark cavern
of their nostrils.

Yet they are cheerful,
so easily entertained.
Each smile, a light
turned on in their faces.

Here is a crowd
with no contagion of appetite.
For that they would need flesh,
through it, to nudge each other
at the slightest notion.

# THEIR HOUSE

They've built an understanding
with their pillars and 2×4s
and the crushed stone that goes into cement,
a way of cutting the dark to fit.
Moths flicker on the shiny, lit surfaces.
There is a border of red and white tulips
and impetuous birds sing. She learns to cook
such things as floating island.
He calls it eggs in snow.

They watch the wind
catch up the narrow yellow leaves
and listen for the knuckle-cracking thunder.
Then great stones begin to roll.
Rain falls. On the side of the woods
it falls again just for them
from the trees, gladly repeating itself.

But one day he notices an orange fungus
twisting over a tree stump.
It reminds him of his childhood, stiff and unreal.
And at night something flings bark and acorns
at the door. The pool,
green with algae, is sinking out of sight.
They forget the bright tanager,
its one note sucked through a straw.
Then no step in her garden
makes anything grow. Then theirs
is not a ship sailing with the wind
but a house with its chimney blown away.

When they leave, boards are knocking,
swollen out of place. Raccoons scratch
in the attic. It is hot and moist

under the rubble of their lives,
ideal conditions for growing. That summer
new owners are moving themselves in.
Younger, quicker. You can see
the sweat on their foreheads.
The woman in her flip-flops shoots ahead.
What does she carry in her arms? Ah,
she is hurrying in to feed their enormous baby.

II

# WHITE HEIFER

The night before my cousin Esther died
my mother dreamt of a white heifer.
There was no twisted metal
in her dream, no back seat
from which to lead the calf to safety.
My mother was pregnant with me then.
I was an eyelash on the back of her hand
that wouldn't blow away, not the favored girl.
She'd never have her back, not even
in the wish of a name. She spoke of her
from the dim doorway of my room,
nearly stumbling over the loss,
like a leg she could not touch down on.
I was saying my prayers, one after another
as if undoing buttons.
She stood in her nightgown, wringing her hands
that glistened with rose-scented cream.
I knew by then that this was how
she got her information,
so much of her life spent
in the shell of a dream.
Then she went to take her place
in the twin bed beside my father's
where he lay, sweat darkening his sheets.
And we slept like voyagers in boats,
they in front, so much farther along
than I. I knew she had come to say
that love is no protection,
and it is easier to speak with love of the dead.

# HOW WE LEARNED

*1. Second Nature*

We were born in the year
of the rabbit. We came into
a world of scrubbed white
interiors, of near transparency,
like a pill at the back
of the mouth, already
beginning to dissolve.
Life found us crouching
between earth and heaven.
Witness our constant search
for cover, the small, imploring eyes
so utterly alive. It's why
we hesitate,
my own narrow width
shivering like silver.

*2. Kisses*

The mother drew the little girl
to her. She took in her hands
the burden of the child's round face.
Then she fastened
her lips to the forehead
as if she were sucking
the poison from a wound. Afterward,
she spat over her shoulder. From this
the child learned. Often
she came and begged at her skirts, "Mommy,
kiss the bad away." And the mother
did. But it was never gone.

3. *Once*

A family lived a perpetual fairy tale.
There were four girls, fresher and prettier
each one by turn, and a boy

who was freckled and sturdy,
growing slightly apart. Yet they all
folded so sweetly one over another,
petals of a flower that knows
instinctively what it is doing,
that closes over itself like a fist.

4. *Daylight Ghosts*

A teenager, I am by this time
used to morning. My clothes
have been laid out
and are waiting for the life
to step back into them.
My friend picks me up for school
at the trolley stop in her first car,
a light blue Rambler, that
once or twice has run off
on its own. The early sun
dazzles the storefronts
and all the silent, witless houses.
We park a minute by the stone church steps,
then, at the holy font,
splash at each other a blessing
that I know would freshen even the dead,
and we are on our way.

## 5. Junior Business Training

He was an only child.
His father, who was perfect,
hoped to turn him
into something fine.
The high school business teacher
knew what was expected.
He had the class
race twice around the room
to turn in their additions. This boy
was always first. Later, in a closet,
he'd wait among the suits,
gray silk, pinstripe, so many
but one cut to all.
He might put out a foot or hand
like clay, like any soft material,
surprised to see it moving
by itself. In the midst
of his father's smell,
destined to be his,
he'd wait, and when the man
had finished shaving,
point at him the small, dear pistol,
his protection,
aim for dear life and shoot.

## 6. Daughter of Patience

She puts on a raincoat and walks
into November. She cannot
contain herself. Breathing is only
a way of moving the heavy air
in and out. She waits, but sometime
he is there. He comes from behind
and turns her and turns her

like the stiff figure of a doll.
They walk from train to woods,
dry leaves disintegrating
underfoot. Now she will know
how to feel on such a day,
earth smell and ash smell. An outdoors
she can never come inside from.

That night her mother is waiting
up for her. Rain and the events
of her life have taught the woman
patient accrual. The father
has gone to bed, pillowing
his old concerns. It is
her mother who is up.
Angry as the sea that swallows
the new sea every minute. A mouth
huge in yawns.
Her mother, with her map of dark.
Now, like a spider, she too
can spin a web out of her bowels.

7. *The Bridge*

Earliest love,
you and I approached the vast river
and the bridge that overtook it

like a second thought. For this,
to descend beneath it,
undercutting its power. I found
the flimsy staircase down
and in the tunnel,
our footsteps were lost below
the strong voice of the river.

In that half-light
I made a first appeal to you.
What I remember in response,
a movement of your hand or eyes,
some gesture to satisfy my expectation.

# DAY CARE

"Let me see me," says Blanquita,
pushing the other kids aside.
She moves toward bikes and bright new toys,
whatever the teacher takes out
and later locks away again.
She says it about anything she notices,
a stone or an ant, a scrap of paper
on the floor. "Let me see me,"
bringing herself into the situation twice,
making sure she is there.
How quick things move
from eye to hand to mouth with her.
She will even eat the sand
in the sandbox and must be watched
each time she pulls her hands out
from where they are buried.

At three o'clock the long-haired teacher
goes home to make her wedding dress.
She is dying yards of lace
with tea. Nervous, she waits
in the shadow of the project
for her bus. It comes and she's gone,
leaving Blanquita to the big high-rise.
Its gray walls close around her
like the rim of a hole. "Let me see me,"
she says, crouching in the hall.
Soon her tongue is black
against shiny white teeth.
"Let me see me," and she takes
into her mouth nails, mop strands,
pieces of the soles of her shoes.

It all tastes good. It tastes
the same, like nothing, like the long wait
for the seed of herself to burst.

# SELF-EXAMINATION

He might be tethered
like an animal, kept from where
he wants to be. A big man,
nearing sixty. He sits and sweats,
though the room is air-conditioned.
His mouth a little open, he is reading
the sign on the door marked Radiology.
He is half up to go after her,

thinking of this life
of hers. The lapses in the love –
his love – which cushions it.
The mutilating surgery and drugs
that sting the organism so it
draws back into itself, counterforce
to the disease. Whatever she has suffered
away from him in other rooms.

I pass easily where he
is not allowed. Like her, I'm chilled
in my thin gown. There is
a fineness, a definiteness
to her face. This beauty
is her own decision. A TV screen
plays a loop of film, women circling
their breasts with their fingertips,
women staring into a mirror.

A foam-rubber breast is lying
on a table. Each of us takes it
in turn, like a lump of dough
we must knead smooth. Something solid
stops me. Unyielding, jewel-hard, a pebble
in this mud. Such seeds grow.

I touch the hollow between
my breasts, this emptiness
that is in me a sign of want.
I look at our still-dressed hands.
Watches, rings. What do they have
to do with us? – madly flashing in the light.

# TEN YEARS OLD

– to Susan Rea

Your son describes
the shuddering in his bones
at the harm that comes to animals.

Today he would not sit
in the restaurant, would not eat.
I didn't blame him. Nothing,
not even food, is what it seems
but is promised to something other.

Just as at night his stamps and coins
are lost. The dark
has come collecting them.
Without a light he will not sleep.

He remembers the shaking train
that got him here, how it
plunged you both into the earth,
carried you along with it.

And on his long walk from school
he has learned to strike each pole
he passes gratefully, an axis.

Even at home, the corners vibrate
with the voice of the winds.

In a milk glass vase
where dahlias hunch, he catches
that wildness loose among the petals.
They are pointing, half flying.

Some days, you say,
he'll cough and cough
and, with what might be
the last of his breath,
blow away all that comes to him.

# ST. KEVIN AND THE WOMAN OF DERRYBAWN

At night her soul is alive
like a beating wing. Ah,
to flatten herself against sleep

so she can rise and mix
into stiff dough what patience
is left after two stillbirths
and a husband who drinks.

A whole winter has grown
into the wheat. The sun
has least force then. Snow hardens
the ground that grips the stalks.

Here is resistance, lending the bread
shape and the substance
to satisfy hunger. She gives the dough
a good thwack with her insensible
wooden spoon and drubs it into rounds,

then walks them down the road
to the hell-fired ovens. And soon
the hiss of steam escapes
from each slashed loaf.

When they are done, she draws
her apron over them, chin down
to anchor them. He is approaching her,

a man the shape of other men. She'll miss
his perfect smile, the hands
still white with holiness. For his part,

he has recognized his task.
Sprinkles of holy water here, of prayer there.
A blessing for a chance to taste.

He has, for all the time it takes,
the luxury of wit. This is the saint
who gave a goose eternal youth.

"Good woman, what have you there?"
She's breathed the life into these loaves
and keeps them close. "I hold
in my apron five round stones."

A wild guess. He brings his prayers
to bear. "If they are stones, I pray
that they be bread. And if they're bread
I pray they turn to stone." The hot loaves
harden in her arms. With a sense of the weight
of every word exchanged
in the world, she lets them fall.

# THE YOUNG SUICIDES IN IRELAND

The sky is lined
like someone's forehead,
like a father's.
He could be worried
whether they will stay near
and come and boil
an egg for him
when they are grown.

    For the present,
    the girls wipe the table
    with a new cloth
    and a will to match
    the energy of dirt.
    Then they rush off
    and with the boys
    make their gesture of speed
    in wide arcs through the town,
    past the blocks of houses,
    the streets slowly unwinding.
    They are young.
    They can feel themselves
    moving toward something.

Soon a sister will be married
or this father, scarcely ill,
will die. And after school
will come hard work,
maybe farm work,
or a hard day of no work.
Wild clouds will collect
over the pale, inevitable future.
There will be the car exhaust,
a drowning in a cistern.

A time the passerby,
taking fright,
will stop and try a house
whose door is locked.

    For the present,
    the lives of the young
    stretch over
    a limitless afternoon.
    Alone or in couples
    they enter the tangle of forest
    where rhododendron
    stifles the oak
    with extravagant beauty.
    Their path has been lit
    by the flight of a rabbit.
    They see what it takes
    to step out of the self.

Home to them
is the realm of clean surfaces,
stone and swept wood.
It is stubborn with life.
They cannot shut out
the murmur of voices,
activity scraping a chair
against the floor.
But they are above this
in their rooms, aware only
of the regularity of the rain
dropping from the eaves.
When it stops
they can hear the clock
ticking, tipping them forward.

# FIRE TOWER

Not fire,

what I thought of then,
my millionth stare
at the washed wood floor,

but something. It was second grade.
I was waiting for something to happen,
wishing the fog would burn away
so something more might be revealed,
the feeling like an itch in my stomach

as I walked with my class
eight times a day up and down the sheltered stairs
in the white-tiled tunnel of the fire tower,
speechless and plunged into dark. But that once
I stepped out into commotion in the yard,
blinded by the dazzle.

A girl had fallen, jumping rope.
I could see blanched skin
below the knee and a keyhole opening
and, with the facts I put together, flesh
that had dropped away to bone.

Perhaps my eyes were not meant to go
so deeply into the workings of the body,
to bone that snapped like a stick. People
were piling up in front of me, catapulting,
acrobatic figures. I was not sure
what I'd seen, aware only of the hurt,
concealed, inevitable,
released at last toward its target.

# RUSH HOUR

Odd, the baby's scabbed face peeking over
the woman's shoulder. The little girl
at her side with her arm in a cast,
wearing a plaid taffeta party dress.
The woman herself who is in shorts and sunglasses
among commuters in the underground station. Her body
that sags and tenses at the same time.

The little girl has not once moved
to touch her or to be touched.
Even on the train, she never turns and says,
"Mommy." Sunlight bobs over her blond head
inclining toward the window. The baby
is excited now. "Loo, loo, loo, loo,"
he calls, a wet crescendo. "He's pulling
my hair," the little girl at last cries out.

A kind man comes up the aisle to see
the baby. He stares at those rosettes of blood
and wants to know what's wrong with him.
The woman says a dog bit him. "It must have been
a big dog, then." "Oh, no. A neighbor's little dog."
The man says, "I hope they put that dog to sleep."
The woman is nearly pleading. "It was an accident. He didn't
mean to do it." The conductor, taking tickets,

asks the little girl how she broke her arm.
But the child looks out to the big, shaded houses.
The woman says, "She doesn't like to talk
about that." No one has seen what is behind
her own dark glasses. She pulls the children to her.
Maybe she is thinking of the arm raised over them,
its motion that would begin like a blessing.

# TAKING TAP AT MISS PATERSON'S

Hop-shuffle one,
hop-shuffle two,
little wooden hands on hips –
"We make a present of our hands."

Remember small, fat you
among the twenty little girls
stampeding to the side.
Last, even then. The line has been
undone by you, come away
like a frayed end.

Miss Paterson,
that big, soft pear,
no longer danced.

She could not raise her hand
without a quavering,
first failure of the life in her,
first shy salute to death.

Your teacher was Miss Dot.
She rouged in two round cheeks
to face you with
and never smiled.
You learned from her
to stamp out sparks of feeling
on the floor.

You danced
between the stairs
and locked back door,
a hallway where winds crossed.
No sun had followed you.

"Tap once for yes,
tap twice for no."

You were obedient. You tried.
But even so,
in that near dark,
some vague thing moved against you
with a greater will.

As if they knew,
they had you hide a penny
in each tap
and when you shook a foot,
it rang.

Brush step, brush step.
Still tentative, you try again.
Remember the shiver of baby fat.
Imagine a lively penny
at your toes.

III

## CLOCK MUSEUM

Clepsydra first, water clock,
with its merciless green light.

Next, dragon fire clock,
a burner of incense,
dedicated to time
by Shiga Prefecture.

Then the oil lamp clock,
and noon cannon that focusing sun rays
discharge into the streets.

After that, grandfather clocks
with their weight-powered pendulum
like a golden plum
cheating the ground.

Clocks where time chirps.
Clocks unraveling.

Flower clock. In the wind,
petals of the zinnia
nudged like small, toothed wheels.

Clock of the youngest child,
breathless, unable to catch up,

and love clock. Ourselves,
coiled around desire.

More wonderful mechanisms,
more delicate movements.

Joy, a spring let go slowly.
Malignancy, already threaded through us.
And loss, loss, whose mandolin effect
will not die out.

# TABLEAUX VIVANTS

*— Naples, 1790*

Emma Hart looks out into the glare
of the sea. A fire sea, a revolution
in the tides. It has swept away the king
and queen of France. It is living energy
in search of form, like that fire sea
erupting from Vesuvius,
where William Hamilton has gone and now,
in blackened clothes, bears home antiquities.

Far from the wide lawns and blistering
white daisies of an English summer,
she is not yet Lady Hamilton, only bartered
or bought like any work of art.

The old man's treasure house is as cool
as if it were already under the ground.
Afternoons at Posillipo he pays the boys
to swim. They leap for him like copper porpoises.

But "better than anything in nature" is
his Emma, "good as anything in antique art."
And soon he helps her stage the "attitudes"
she's maker of and sole material.
A bell tolls in the town and she begins
the beautiful realities of twenty seconds.

Sir William holds the light. He's had
a Grecian costume made and with some shawls,
a handkerchief, she draws herself
into the likeness on an ancient coin.
Two-sided like a coin: Emma, his still,
white lily. Lily, stiff on its stem,

until it crumples back to life.
Then, by turn, she's reaching, bent, imploring.
Each posture stopped as it goes forward,
like those at Pompeii, cast in molten rock.

Once she lets down her coiled hair, an emblem
of madness or youth, becomes Cassandra
waving a torch. Illustrious,
aristocratic watchers burn to read
what's written on the oval of her face.

Her lips lock in a smile.
When she turns back to the sea, it is a flare,
a bright blue-green that hurts the eyes.
It promises ships, triumphant Lord Nelson.

In the town, jewel-like flies converge on the market.
The people are clamoring for bread.
It is the feast of San Gennaro, patron saint.
If his dried blood does not liquify,
they must prepare for an era of disaster.

# MIMOSA

It must have been July,
their blossoms just opening,
July, near my birthday.
Red-aureoled,
spread like nipples.
The name, he said, meant beloved.

And though I knew first
through him the tiny
needles of pleasure,
I pretended not to hear.

He looked away
as I changed
in the high stalks of corn.
(Really, I stood
in the shadow
of that word.) Then he led me
into the ocean.

He was thirty. My mother said,
"He won't marry you,"
as if it mattered at all,
boys my age at last
catching up with me.

Mimosa, I thought,
looking down at myself.
Through the hard bark
he'd have heard my heart beating.

# GOODWIFE PLAYING THE VIRGINALS

*— after a painting by de Witte*

The woman's hands are hungry birds.
Here is their breakfast of music.

In the cabin bed her lover lies,
listening. The plucked notes scatter
along the keyboard of his spine.

A mirror returns the room to her,
velvets, red sashes, an earthenware jug.
The small dog, signaling fidelity.

Then a staccato of rectangles.
Who has upset these boxes
of sunlight on the floor?

One by one the ordered rooms open,
each staring into another's face.

Far off, a housemaid sweeps
at the speck in her mind.

Useless now, the man's sword
slung across a chair. The true scourge
is the broom on its hinge,
the maid's stout shoulder.

The man is trapped by the open door.

# STORY IN THE STYLE OF HENRY JAMES

On that beach at Ostia,
a foreign couple lie side by side,
their friend nearby. The sand
is fire hot. Each grain
is a tiny particle of the truth
cut apart so it cannot do any harm.
This is a different sea, not proud,
not galloping. They face
its calm deliberation, the small
scribblings of waves. But soon,
on a boat deck before their eyes,
two fishermen in colorful striped shirts
begin to stalk each other.
One cracks a bottle on the rail.
He holds what's left above him at arm's length
as if he fears it too. A comedy
of gestures. Cries the married couple
barely understand. But the rays
of bright sun combing the water,
that rasp of the sea, and the raised arm
half the beach away, they understand.
The friend has met them on a train
or on the plane coming over.
So little money left she'd sleep
on a pillow in their bathtub
if they let her. How to explain
the wife's strange refusal?
The day is heating up. The sand
draws to their moist and reddened skin
a blossoming irritation.
The men's shouts twist in the air,
uneven as the cries of gulls.
Now everyone around is watching too.
Only the eyes move, their bodies

are warm stone. The friend must look away.
The wife cannot. She sees in the boat
her light little rental apartment
where the furniture is dancing. She's there
making curtains. "God of enclosures,"
she murmurs, "God of risks.
Give us at least this net of lace."

# "LITTLE RAY OF SUNSHINE"

*"A stolen glance at Lina Basquette, her face flickering with the light from her own image" — from Barry Parks's* NEW YORKER *profile*

One minute you are a little girl
shuffling your feet on the counter
as your druggist father dispenses
Ex-Lax and tooth powder, the record salesman
watching you mime Nellie Melba, something
from Puccini. At nine you are Pavlova, Jr.,
in silent featurettes. Outside,
it's California. It almost never rains.
When it does, there's the sound
of the whole world breaking apart.

Your father is Old South and proud.
He mixes up a powder on the swaying
metal scales. By sunrise he's gone.
Then, stage mother or poor widow, she keeps
you on your toes. The simple, truthful title
of the film you're dancing through
is "Shoes." You're ten and typed
as an exotic. "A Romany Rose,"
"The Black Mantilla" next. They like it
that although a child, you never smile.

"The Godless Girl" will be your greatest part,
the one you are remembered for.
She is a high school atheist. At sixteen
you're featured by the Follies.
It's California. The ocean hurls itself
and hurls itself. How you are loved.
Seven partners in your marriage dance.
You date the Crown Prince of Albania,
even Hitler himself. Once you decide

to celebrate. No one knows
this is a farewell party. Anyhow,
the dosage is too small. It's California.
The sun falls across a face,
changing even the color of the eyes,
one dark, the other pale gold, as if
the child were that eager to please.

# WHY YOUR FATHER CRIED

Your sister is telling the story. It was
June, the year he died. They are on
the porch. The wisteria curves around,
making what is said seem a secret. Your father
is an old man. There is so much to remember.
She can see that he is crying. How can she not
feel sad, somewhat peripheral? She is beside him
but a memory of you has kindled him to tears.
You had a paper route. You got up in the dark.
Snow might be falling. Your squat, little boy's
hands rolled and twisted the papers into logs
that you piled in the basket of your bike.
Then you buttoned your heavy coat. All your motions
carried the stiffness of sleep and inexperience.
Your father stood watching from a doorway. He wanted
to go to you and stop you, to send you back
to bed. He'd take the papers for you in his car.
But no, regret would be a door to duty. He let you go.

Your mother, who has been pouring tea, looks up.
"It wasn't you," she says. "Of course, he loved you
awfully well. But he was crying for himself."
She is thinking how his mother must have felt,
waking him for work, nudging him into a consciousness
of six younger brothers and sisters. She passes
the thin china cups. Grains of rice are fired into them
where the light shines through. Their bottoms
and rims and the underlying saucers all are edged
with a pattern like blue bridges, like the letter "H"
circling around. You pick yours up and hold it
toward you, drinking. Maybe you see the word "I"
pointing to you many times, "I," "I," "I," "I," and so
you speak. "Couldn't he see that I wanted to go –
under my own steam – away from the house

and what he gave me? I wonder what I was thinking,
out, like that, in the dark. I know they were
some of the best thoughts I had in my life."

# WHAT THE OLD SAY

Aloe,
aloe vera,
broken and weeping.
You heal small wounds,
then make yourself whole again

while for me
there is the danger even
of taking
a few unguarded steps,

so, like skaters,
my ladyfriends and I
link arms, not knowing
what to expect of the day

and whispering, go
first one way, then another
as if through trees,
careful that the trees
do not brush us too deeply.

Odd, then, how Alice
drew back from that chain of arms.

Was it fear
of contracting a hopeless disease –
life? – and broke dates
and kept the two daily miles
still in her shoes
and even the telephone
was too short a cord
to anyone.

From her apartment
I could hear the piano
go on correcting itself,
though the piano has limits

but I understood
because there are afternoons
that grind me down to something else,
to a state of dust
that I stamp into
everyone else's life.

I should add,
when weather keeps us in,
we may gather in one small room
and listen to the rain
that is like the sound of a door opening
from time to time
into a crowded street.

# DOWN THE STREET

"How's my darlingest girl?" Mr. D.
says to my friend from down the street,
his next door neighbor. She is pretty
and spoiled, no reason not be to.
I have noticed that she never washes
her hands when she pees, that
her mother treats her hair with olive oil
to make it shine. I wish I could share
in the light surrounding her,
I wish Mr. D.'s big, heavy arm would
fall over my shoulders with the same choice.

This is the summer I can sing all the songs
on the Hit Parade. And I have learned to dance
recklessly in my friend's basement
where we throw each other against the walls,
signaling for spins and turns with pushes
of our hands. We couple and uncouple
like cars in a moving train. Then in
a kissing game or as a dare,
that bewildered boy, Earl,
eyes dark as sealed windows, rubs his mouth
against mine, such odd surfaces touching
but for the heat, like tree bark and glass.

# IN THE BINDERY

The shift begins. Metal clanks
against metal. It's the sound
of a thousand Houdinis shackling
themselves. Over this, the women
go on talking. They understand
each other well enough.
"I fell down the stairs. I had
to have it fixed." The other
can't help wondering if her husband
broke her nose. If she had
the operation for her looks.
She's a student. This is
real life to her, this summer job,
while Lena's here for good.
All night the two step out
in small, one-sided pirouettes.
They lift the paper onto
its cradle on the belt, where it
will be trimmed and stapled
farther on. At each step
something is added or taken away.
The steel hands meet unhurriedly,
over and over, at right angles.
The women count on this and on
the short dead points that come
in anyone's life. "Chicken,"
Lena calls. "Don't work
so hard. They don't give medals
here." It's true her muscles ache.
This is the first time they've
been put to any use. She feels
the sweat that stands out
on her forehead like a seal.
Lena is staring straight ahead,

gray eyes like two clear lights.
These were machines, you never
tempted them. Where they held
and supported, they could crush.
The metal rings with force and clarity.
Sometimes it seems to have
a change of heart but then goes on.

# THE CARDINAL

Again this morning I woke
as the cardinal banged
his head against the window,
slowly, purposefully, like
someone knocking. He does it
not to harm himself – we're sure
of this. He is only cracking
seeds for food. Or it may be
an accident. Witness
the bruises on my elbows,
my scratched hands. I myself
have no sense of where I begin
or end, like that dim lilac bush

that goes involuntarily
forward. You planted it
for someone else, without much sun
or hope. And if it didn't root,
well, one plant will always
take over from another. But it made
a thin connection here. I'd miss
that fragrance at the kitchen door.
Sometimes I find it upstairs too
in the deep closets where
her dresses hung. My own idea
about the cardinal is,
he's fighting for his life.
He sees an enemy, not just
that pale reflection in the glass.

IV

# LATERNA MAGICA

What you remember
from the dark theater in Prague
is more than an image,
less than real life. Nothing
you have exactly experienced.
Trompe l'oeil fruit
on a tabletop. Violins played
by unseen hands.

Later, at work,
you are presented with disaster
after disaster. A motorcycle
rams the side of a car
returning someone's teenage son
from a party. You picture him,
curly haired and singing,
arm stretched out along the seat,
embracing dark. His twin
will not leave the hospital
without seeing the body
no one could still
mistake for his.
You have noticed for the first time
the speech impediment
of the man who tells the story,
how his tongue
pulls back from the words.

And one day
a house burns down
as a woman cooks dinner.
Miraculous – the family escapes.
Expensive place. Acres
of feathery trees. You know the man,

have in your mind a glimpse of him
as you turned a corner
or at a blind landing of the stairs.
You forget this fire
until a plane crash lands
and he and his child are listed
among the lost. Their names
could be tubas and kettledrums,

a music too important
for the radio. Pink messages
pulse across your desk
but you are staring
at the irises in a vase
that rise like faces out of smoke.

# OFFICES

I think of days
with numbers hung on them
and times scratched in.
Of Abigail,
who'd taken clerical,
evening the stacks of paper,
hands just loose enough
to let the sheets find
their own way to a straight edge.
I'd wished I could let
things go like that.

In the black church
I watched her marry, the pale gowns
sent down the aisles
like flowers floated on water.
That world, a photo negative.
I was a ghost, a smudge
of nothing happening. Otherwise
we were the same. Set up
on thin high heels
the same fine bodies. They worked for us
like new machines.

I don't worry about her.
She had such careful hands. She'd be
a good shuffler of cards. Her mother
cleaned our offices.
"A looker in her day," the old white men,
our bosses, said. And who were they
to judge the death of beauty,
cold limbs leaning into us
as they pulled us to the dance floor
at the holiday party?

## THE SPELL

How tired I was, and I slept
from my twelfth birthday
until I was nearly eighteen.
A hot, rosy sleep, punctuated
by menstrual blood.

The booty of dreams,
the plaid silk dress that I loved,
and perfume bottles
won for my drawings
of long-haired dogs.

I could not have heard
the summer-loud insects
pluck at the screens
or the gathering of rain
as others did and been afraid.

The thin light of the house
shone in my eyes
but did not wake me.

I climbed to a room
papered with princesses.
There I lay down where birds slept
and fish, and the very crumbs
that could have told the way
out of the wilderness of sleep

slept. Sometime I rose
and left this cave of dark,
going out into the true dark
of the streets, of a boy's arms.

How had it planted itself
in my cells, this sleep?
Settling over me as snow settles
over mountains and winter rivers.
As my heavy knee-length hair
had settled over me
when I was a child.

# STRAWBERRY FÊTE

At the hospital grounds that night
the cranky mechanisms flowered,
the eccentric circle of the ferris wheel,
the wheel of fortune spinning a gaudy future.
A poor fair but it would shine under the eyes
of the dying. Strangers brought simple,
unnamable faces. Neighbors lightened their step
and fell back from the web
that night and day surrounded us.

Even those for whom it was difficult came:
pale Marie, her widowed father's right arm.
Ahead, her redhaired sister
pulsed like a star. Marie, failed nun.
In the long days in the dark house
she'd bend to wash the floors
as once she had dropped to her knees
with the weight of the Holy Spirit.

Now, here, it was hard to believe
that the same moonlight splashed over our houses,
those rows of houses snapping shut at dusk.
Not a word that didn't echo,
that would not shake the walls.
So you went the next night and the next,
as if all year you'd been starving
for the thick whipped cream like a froth of hope
and the perfect strawberries.

# SPORTS PHOTOGRAPHER

*— for Jim Drake*

As a young man he ran. He knew
that the slapping of feet
is a natural language to the earth.
Then, in a sprint, his knee turned in.

After that, it was his eye that moved,
inching forward. The camera
became a part of him, tough pulsebeats
advancing like the blood.

He began to anticipate.
If a ball through a hoop
is a wish personified, it's his wish too.
He looks for symmetry, a promise that's made
in muscle and bone.

But sometimes he can see
that the organs will make the move, off center
like gritty magnets.

Maybe he'll focus on
someone who's lost this element,
the old-time baseball pro,
"yanked-out, disappointed, bent."

He has a feel for finishes.
He will pay out a hundred rolls of film
on deserted fields in the natural light
of summer afternoons,

or slow the speed at the end of the race
so that the runners appear to bloom
into a wide, deserved sleep.

For years he has been looking for
a vest with so many pockets
he can never run out of film.

# DEATH SITE

Cluster of blue
and gray striped feathers,
the hollow center of the act,
what has transpired
in the silent dark
out of the sun
of anyone's witnessing.

Nor could my eyes
have stopped it. Nothing
of the valiant organs or call
that tempts the creature
out of itself. No visible death,
no plan, not self-inflicted
harm, collision of matter.

The wet leaves,
the white dirt, clear
of incident. What can I do
but reconstruct it
from myself, tentative
in this life, creature
to sit and be silent?
The light gains strength.
Each ruined wisp
intensified to color,
signaling.

# GIFT OF FLOWERS

Thunder, unheard all winter,
the sound of harm.

She stands at the screen door
exhaling cigarette smoke,
and looks out toward the next yard
at larkspur, full-blown poppies,
roses spinning out of control.

She is thinking,
people give you flowers

as if they were a prize. Each,
an extravagant badge
turned to the light. When really
it is only a small corpse on a stem.

If he gives her flowers,
it is so they can die in her house.
There is a first scream
of color, a scent
that robs her of breath.
Then the bloating, the widening.

In the end she is reminded
of how the dancer mimes rage,
like a poisoned bush,
close to the ground and shaking.

# RIVER BATHERS

This was no paradise.
The road bristled with ferns.
A tree threw its shape, headfirst
out of the shadows, so I saw
that there was water. We undressed
and went in. The human smell
fell away. Our limbs moved out
from the hub of the body,
so simply connected. Our skin
was a jumping-off place for light.
You could make a moral of this,
like the dazzle spinning off
Prometheus's hand: that water
completes us, that without it,
an animal is dust. From the far shore

rose factories and resplendent dumps.
I held up my head. I scissor-kicked,
remembering to take in breath enough
to get me through. Climbing out,
I passed bushes and vines
looking themselves as if they had just
stepped out of the water. And on
the closest lawns, strange flowers,
cannas and dark dahlias, circled
the grass and rusting iron furniture.

# FOR ONE WHO CAME LATE TO POETRY

Not someone I knew well, not close,
our connection was remote. I don't
know why you tell me this. Crumpling
to the ground? Someplace distant. There was
grass, you say. A Roman aqueduct. Small woman,
doll-like, with her tiny, cinched waist.
But nothing, if not strong. Tensile strength
of a dancer. I remember it as apple red
or blue, that velvet dress she wore.
Determined. Her life constructed,
I don't know, with purpose,
like an aqueduct. Ironic, that old accident.
The jolt that shook her free. She, pulled up
at a gas pump. The other car, out of control.
Tinnitus. It left her more alone. She was
not young. My age. Remote. What brought us
together – a new mortar – was poetry. But it
was chaos in her life. Anything solid
showed its weakness, came undone. Tinnitus.
The delicate, spiraling ear.
Signals changed place, far voices
overpowering her. The near were mute.
Balance too was lost. And by this time,
motherhood, that language of dependency,
was gone. We'd met once at a bus stop. They,
like a small band of primates. Mother, father.
Bright children, though not, at that time,
pretty. One picked his nose. Then she,
alone with them, they falling onto her body.
Roman aqueduct. In pictures it resembles
a structure of fists. Poetry allowed her
darkness. A labyrinth and a surprise.
Eccentric arrangements of the furniture,
everything a grown woman wants.

# BADGERS

I had been told not to approach them
as they go at dusk over the fields
for worms and mice. Aware of me
the male might attack, holding me off
while the others escaped. But these three
or four, I have no fear of. They are
my own dark creatures, come with me
through the fields, shadows I have brought,
whatever feeds on the start of night.

BORN in Philadelphia in 1939, Elaine Terranova grew up in a working class neighborhood and has lived in that city ever since. She has held a variety of jobs, including temp worker and copy-editor, as well as instructor in English and Creative Writing at Temple University and reading and writing specialist at Community College of Philadelphia.

Terranova's first book, *The Cult of the Right Hand* (Doubleday), was chosen by Rita Dove as the winner of the 1990 Walt Whitman Award from the Academy of American Poets. Her poems have appeared in *The New Yorker*, *The American Poetry Review*, *Boulevard*, *Confrontations*, and other magazines. *Damages* is her second book.

BOOK DESIGN and composition by John D. Berry, using Adobe PageMaker 6.0 and a Power Computing Power 120. The type is Quadraat, an original digital typeface designed by Fred Smeijers and released in 1992 by FontShop International as part of their FontFont type library. Quadraat displays the subtle irregularities of a handmade face, which make it particularly readable at small sizes and give it a distinctive character at large sizes. Printed by McNaughton & Gunn.